STARS OF PRO WRESTLING

★ ★ ★ ★ ★ ★ ★ ★ ★ ★

John Cena

BY TIM O'SHEI

Consultant:
Mike Johnson, Writer
PWInsider.com

Capstone press®

Mankato, Minnesota

Edge Books are published by Capstone Press,
151 Good Counsel Drive, P.O. Box 669, Mankato, Minnesota 56002.
www.capstonepress.com
Copyright © 2010 by Capstone Press, a Capstone Publishers company.

Library of Congress Cataloging-in-Publication Data
O'Shei, Tim.
    John Cena / by Tim O'Shei.
    p. cm. — (Edge books. Stars of pro wrestling)
    Includes bibliographical references and index.
    Summary: "Describes the life and career of pro wrestler John Cena"—
Provided by publisher.
    ISBN 978-1-4296-3347-5 (library binding)
    1. Cena, John — Juvenile literature. 2. Wrestlers — United States —
Biography — Juvenile literature. 3. Motion picture actors and actresses —
United States — Biography — Juvenile literature. I. Title.
GV1196.C46O74 2010
796.812092 — dc22
[B]
                                                    2008055926

Editorial Credits
Angie Kaelberer, editor; Ted Williams, designer; Jo Miller, media researcher

Photo Credits
Alamy/Allstar Picture Library, 5
Getty Images Inc./AFP/Tiziana Fabi, 19; Kevin Winter, 11; Lucas Dawson,
    12; WireImage/Denise Truscello, 16; WireImage/Don Arnold, cover, 24,
    25; WireImage/Jamie McCarthy, 15; WireImage/Nick Doan, 28
Globe Photos/John Barrett, 9, 18; Milan Ryba, 6, 23
Newscom/AFP/Tiziana Fabi, 26; Giovanni, 20
Supplied by Capital Pictures, 27

Design Elements
Shutterstock/amlet; Henning Janos; J. Danny; kzww

012010
005677R

TABLE OF CONTENTS

Chapter 1

FIGHTING UNTIL THEY QUIT

Pro wrestler John Cena was already a champion. Now he had to prove he deserved it.

It was May 22, 2005. The event was Judgment Day. John was facing John Bradshaw Layfield, better known as JBL. One month earlier, at WrestleMania, John had won the World Wrestling Entertainment (WWE) Championship belt from JBL. John wanted his belt to be unique. He ditched the regular belt and instead had one made that featured a spinning gold logo in the middle. Meanwhile, JBL took back the original belt and claimed the title was his.

That set up the Judgment Day showdown. John had to show everyone that he was the one and only champion. The rules of the match were simple. John and JBL would fight until one of them said, "I quit!"

John had to prove he deserved the WWE Championship.

JBL put John in a chokehold during their battle for the title.

The match started with a bang. John rode into the arena on the back of a semitruck that shot steam and fireworks into the air. JBL entered the arena in a limousine. A deejay blared hip-hop music from a turntable. Those beats soon gave way to a beating on both sides.

John bodyslammed JBL at ringside. JBL smashed John with a chair. John continued fighting. The battle continued atop the limousine. JBL tried to choke John with a cord. John wriggled away. How much more would John be able to take?

WRESTLING FACT

John works out every day, no matter where his matches take him. He can bench-press 450 pounds (204 kilograms).

Chapter 2

TOUGH FROM THE START

John Felix Anthony Cena proved he was tough from the moment he was born on April 23, 1977. His umbilical cord was wrapped around his neck three times. Doctors were worried that he would suffer brain damage from the lack of oxygen. But as John's father said years later, John cried hard. For a baby, that's a sign of health. That's not much different from a wrestler. Masters of the ring need big mouths too. It's no wonder that John Cena became a pro wrestling superstar.

John proved he was strong from the start.

COMPETITIVE BROTHERS

John grew up in West Newbury, Massachusetts. He was the second oldest of five boys born to John Cena Sr. and Carol Cena. John and his brothers played basketball, football, and baseball. Of course, they wrestled too. John liked to pretend he was heavyweight champ Hulk Hogan.

The Cena boys watched professional wrestling every Saturday night with their father. In fact, wrestling was the only reason John Sr. even bought cable TV service.

NEVER BLENDING IN

As a kid, John liked to stand out from the crowd. He wore T-shirts with cartoonlike characters and weird sayings. He shaved his hair into a Mohawk. One time, he was supposed to make a music video for a school assignment. Instead, John made a bloody horror film.

Because John was different, he was singled out. Other kids beat him up. John was skinny and had a hard time defending himself. One year, John asked for a weight set for Christmas. John worked out every day. Around age 15, he joined a local fitness center called Hard Nock's Gym. Owner Dave Nock trained him, pushing John to handle heavier weights and different lifts.

Hulk Hogan (right) was one of John's favorite wrestlers when he was a kid.

John has been building EX BRAND his muscles since he was in high school.

Soon, John was no longer a skinny kid. His muscles were rippled and chiseled. He decided to enter bodybuilding competitions. But John was embarrassed to show himself in the tiny bathing suit bodybuilders wear. Nock had a solution. He had John put on the suit and then took him to the main traffic circle in town. There, with a constant flow of cars passing by, Nock made John strike nearly a dozen bodybuilder poses. That kicked John's embarrassment. He was ready to compete.

Top Competitor

John did well in competitions of any sort, whether it was bodybuilding or his other favorite sport, football. John played football at his high school, Cushing Academy. He continued as an offensive lineman at Springfield College in Springfield, Massachusetts. He worked out morning, afternoon, and evening. John was usually the first player on the football field for practice. Afterward, it was rare that anyone stayed on the field later than he did. Before games, John charged up his teammates with pep talks. During games, he was the team's leader on the field.

John studied exercise **physiology** in college. He wanted to be a personal trainer. To do it, he needed to complete a six-month internship. After graduating from college, John moved to Southern California to do the internship and start his career. He did start his career — but it wasn't the one he had planned on.

physiology — the study of how the body works

Chapter 3

THE PROTOTYPE

John had never lost his love for wrestling. In college, he watched WWE's *Raw* on Monday nights. Once, John was supposed to be in the main event of a charity wrestling match. Most of his friends were treating the wrestling event as a noncompetitive show. Not John. He trained by bodyslamming his friends and giving them *piledrivers*. The show ended up getting canceled, but John would have been ready if it had happened.

John's wrestling dreams got a boost in California. One day at the gym, wrestlers Mike and Mark Bell came up to talk to him. They told John he should give pro wrestling a try. John took the wrestlers' advice. Soon, he was competing in the Ultimate Pro Wrestling (UPW) league in Southern California.

John never lost his dream of
being a pro wrestler.

WRESTLING MOVE

piledriver — a wrestler holds the opponent upside
down by the legs and slams the opponent to the mat

Randy Orton (left) and John both wrestled in OVW.

THE PROTOTYPE

John was known as "The **Prototype**." He bleached his hair blond and wore sunglasses in the ring.

Wrestling in UPW wasn't glamorous. After every match, John and the other wrestlers would help break down the ring and pack it up for the next event in another city. Then John would drive home, which usually took him a couple of hours. He would get up early the next morning to go to his job, work out, and head to another match at night. For all this, he was making only $40 or $50 per match.

Even though John was in a small-time league, he was developing a big-time reputation. Jim Ross, who scouted wrestlers for WWE, flew to California to watch John. Ross signed John to a **developmental contract**. John started competing for Ohio Valley Wrestling (OVW), based in Kentucky. OVW was a feeder system for WWE. Other future stars like Batista and Randy Orton wrestled there too.

prototype — an original or early model of something

developmental contract — a deal to compete in a smaller league as a way to train for a bigger league

John used humor in the ring. He taunted opponents by comparing them to characters from movies like *Back to the Future* and *Star Wars*. He made funny references to TV shows and musicians. John even started rapping in the ring. He put on a good show. Most important of all, he was a tough, athletic wrestler. After he signed John, Ross told WWE owner Vince McMahon that John would someday headline WrestleMania.

John used his humor and rapping skills in the ring.

He's Got the Moves

Like all wrestlers, John has his own signature moves he uses in the ring. For the Attitude Adjuster, he lifts his opponent to his shoulders and then falls forward, slamming the opponent's back to the mat. For the STF, he drops onto the opponent's back and wraps his arms around the opponent's head before pulling back. When an opponent is down, or sometimes even before he's down, John waves the back of his hand in front of the other wrestler's face. This is called the You Can't See Me. Shortly before John finishes off an opponent, he often bends over to pump up his shoes. Then he stands straight and pumps his hands up and down by his thighs. This move is called the Five Knuckle Shuffle.

One of John's moves is called the You Can't See Me.

John uses parts of his own personality in his wrestling character.

RUTHLESS AGGRESSION

On June 27, 2002, John got his first big shot in WWE. John faced former Olympic gold medalist Kurt Angle. When asked why he felt he deserved a shot at WWE, John responded, "Ruthless aggression!" This was a phrase that Vince McMahon used. John vowed to meet McMahon's challenge and be ruthless in the ring. He lost his first match to Angle but showed enough talent to win a spot in WWE.

In WWE, John dropped the Prototype personality. He wrestled under his real name, which is fairly rare in wrestling. John's character was a rapping wrestler. He dressed in cutoff jean shorts, pump-up sneakers, and old-time sports jerseys. John looked and sounded like a guy who could win a rap battle on any sidewalk. But once the bell rang, he became a wrestler — one bound for the top.

WRESTLING FACT

All WWE wrestlers have music that plays when they enter a ring. But John is the only one who performs his own entrance theme. The rap song is called *The Time is Now*.

Chapter 4

REACHING THE TOP

The WWE Championship. The United States Championship. The Tag Team Championship. John has won each of these belts multiple times. Whether he's wrestling, rapping, or acting, John puts on a great show.

"I QUIT!"

The way John ended the 2005 Judgment Day match against JBL shows his spectacular style. John grabbed JBL and hurled him into a TV set. He then shoved JBL's head through one of the limousine windows. The fight moved to John's truck. John ripped an exhaust pipe from the truck and ran toward JBL. "I quit!" JBL screamed as John used the pipe to shove him through a wall. With those words, the match was over. John was still the WWE champion.

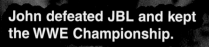
John defeated JBL and kept
the WWE Championship.

GETTING "EDGE-Y"

One of John's most famous **feuds** was in 2006 against Edge. The pair battled with words, fists, and finally, furniture! On September 17, 2006, John wrestled Edge in a Tables, Ladders, and Chairs (TLC) match. The wrestlers could use tables, chairs, and a ladder as weapons. The only way to win the match was to climb atop the 16-foot (5-meter) ladder and grab Edge's WWE Championship belt. The belt was hanging about 20 feet (6 meters) above the ring.

feud — a long-running quarrel

Edge was John's opponent during a TLC match at Unforgiven in 2006.

John needed to keep Edge from reaching the championship belt.

After trading whacks and smacks, Edge hit the mat long enough for John to set up the ladder in the ring. John started climbing toward the belt. The belt was almost in his reach when wrestler Lita ran into the ring. She tipped the ladder, knocking John over the top ropes and through a table outside the ring. Then Edge started climbing the ladder, but John got back into the ring. Lita slammed a chair into John's back. The blow pushed John into the ladder, which toppled over.

The back-and-forth action continued until both wrestlers were climbing the ladder. They reached the top at the same time. John settled the standoff by lifting Edge onto his shoulders. He then gave him an Attitude Adjuster. Edge crashed through two tables that were stacked next to the ladder. John grabbed the belt and held it high. He was not only on top of the ladder, he was on top of the wrestling world. John was the WWE champion!

John celebrated winning the WWE Championship once again.

John Goes Hollywood

Many wrestlers have tried show business over the years. John is one of the latest to give it a shot. In 2005, he released a hip-hop CD called *You Can't See Me*. The next year, he starred in an action movie called *The Marine*.

John decided to take part in the movie after visiting American troops in Iraq and Afghanistan. His family worried that he would be hurt, but John wanted to help the soldiers in any way he could. "Get home safe," he told the troops. "Get home soon. Y'all are the real heroes."

John did many of his own stunts in *The Marine*.

Make-a-Wish Champion

John donates much of his time to the Make-A-Wish Foundation. Make-A-Wish grants wishes for kids with serious illnesses. Often that wish is to meet a favorite sports or Hollywood star. Since 2004, John has granted an average of 25 wishes a year. He was honored in 2008 when he hit the 100-wish mark. When he accepted the award, John set himself a much higher goal. "We'll have the real celebration," he said, "when we hit 1,000."

John granted a wish to young fan Max Arizona in 2008.

JOHN'S FUTURE

John could remain one of wrestling's biggest stars for several years. The biggest challenge for any wrestler is to remain healthy. John has dealt with injuries in the past. In 2007, his right pectoral muscle in his chest was torn from the bone when he hiptossed Mr. Kennedy. The next year, John hurt his neck during a SummerSlam match against Batista. The injury required surgery and several months of recovery. In November 2008, though, John returned to the ring. At Survivor Series, he defeated Chris Jericho for the World Heavyweight Championship.

No matter how long John wrestles, his ability as a showman will give him the chance to stay in the spotlight. As long as he can make people cheer and laugh, John Cena will be a star.

WRESTLING FACT

John's personality has made him a popular guest on TV shows. He's appeared on *Jimmy Kimmel Live*, *Late Night with Conan O'Brien*, *MADtv*, *Saturday Night Live*, and *Larry King Live*.

GLOSSARY ★ ★ ★ ★ ★ ★

charity (CHAYR-uh-tee) — a group that raises money or collects goods to help people in need

developmental contract (duh-VEHL-up-ment-tuhl KAHN-tract) — a deal in which a wrestler is paid to compete in a smaller league as a way to train for a bigger league like WWE

feud (FYOOD) — a long-running quarrel between two people or groups of people

internship (in-TURN-ship) — a temporary job in which a person works with and learns from experienced workers

physiology (fiz-ee-OL-uh-jee) — the study of how the body works

prototype (PROH-tuh-tipe) — an original or early model of something

signature move (SIG-nuh-chur MOOV) — the move for which a wrestler is best known; this move is also called a finishing move.

READ MORE

Grayson, Robert. *John Cena*. Modern Role Models. Philadelphia: Mason Crest, 2009.

O'Shei, Tim. *Batista*. Stars of Pro Wrestling. Mankato, Minn.: Capstone Press, 2010.

Shields, Brian, and Kevin Sullivan. *WWE Encyclopedia.* New York: DK Publishing, 2009.

INTERNET SITES

FactHound offers a safe, fun way to find Internet sites related to this book. All of the sites on FactHound have been researched by our staff.

Here's all you do:

Visit *www.facthound.com*

FactHound will fetch the best sites for you!

INDEX ★ ★ ★ ★ ★ ★ ★